Women Empowerment Government Programmes Perspective

Women Empowerment Government Programmes Perspective

Dr. Karanam Viswa Bhushan

KALPAZ

First Published, 2020
Published by

Kalpaz Publications
C-30, Satyawati Nagar,
Delhi – 110052
Ph.: 011-47034999, 9811692060
www.kalpazpublications.com
E-mail: kalpaz@hotmail.com

Printed at: Gyan Press, Delhi.

Cataloging in Publication Data—DK
Courtesy: D.K. Agencies (P) Ltd. <docinfo@dkagencies.com>

Bhushan, Karanam Viswa, 1963- **author.**
Women empowerment government programmes perspective / Dr. Karanam Viswa Bhushan.
pages cm
Includes bibliographical references and index.
ISBN 9789353246044 (HB)

1. Women in development—Ethiopia. 2. Women—Government policy—Ethiopia. I. Title.

LCC HQ1240.5.E8B48 2021 | DDC 305.420963 23

Acknowledgements

First of all, I would like to thank the Almighty God for his everlasting heavenly blessings.

I would like to extend my special thanks and profound appreciation to my student Nhial Khat Dor who has contributed for the successful completion of the research work.

I would like to thank the women of Makuey Woreda Gambella region who participated and cooperated during the research work.

I would like to extend my thanks to all the heads and staff of the Offices of Women Children Affair (WCA), Makuey woreda Education (MWE), Woreda administration Office (MWAO), Woreda 01 Kebele and Woreda 02 Kebele.

I would like to express my heartfelt thanks to my dear brother.

Prof. K. Pushpanadham and his family for their support and encouragement.

I would like to express my deep sense of gratitude to my beloved parents and family members for unending inspiration and encouragement.

Contents

List of Tables

Chapterone

Introduction

1.1 Background of the Study

Women empowerment is believed to be an important factor in determining the utilization of child health practices. When women are empowered, children thrive, and the countries flourish reaping a double dividend for women and children (Former UN secretary Kofi A. Annan). Women's empowerment and gender equality concepts are important in fostering health and human development. Empowerment describes the process of change where an individual with prior inability to choose has the access and freedom to make choices (Kabeer, 2005).

1.2 The Global Context

It is noted that, 70% of women in the world's population are poor. Women constitute almost half of the world's population but are discriminated in various spheres of life. Everywhere in the world; it is mostly women who are responsible for their family's food security and nutritional balance. However, women and girls are still facing discrimination when it comes to accessing and controlling food from the production to the consumption stage, improving their livelihoods, and accessing education and healthcare. Women empowerment refers to increasing the spiritual, political, social, educational, gender or economic strength of individuals and communities of women. Women's empowerment in India is heavily dependent on many different variables that include geographical location (urban / rural) educational status social status (caste and class) and age. Policies on

Women's empowerment exist at the national, state and local (Panchayat) levels in many sectors, including health, education, economic opportunities, and gender based violence and political participation. However, there are significant gap between policy advancements and actual practice at the community level.

Empowerment of women is essentially the process of up liftmen of economic, social and political status of women, the traditionally underprivileged ones, in the society. It is the process of guarding them against all forms of violence. Women empowerment involves the building up of a society, a political environment, wherein women can breathe without the fear of oppression, exploitation, apprehension, discrimination and the general feeling of persecution, which goes with being a woman in a traditionally male dominated structure.

Women constitute almost 50% of the world's population but India has shown disproportionate sex ratio whereby female's population has been comparatively lower than males. As far as their social status is concerned, they are not treated as equal to men in all the places. In the Western societies, the women have got equal right and status with men in all walks of life. But gender disabilities and discriminations are found in India even today (Khan and Noreen 2012).

Historically demonstrates that out of all deprived groups in the world, women have suffered the most. Their suffering knew no bounds based on culture, race, region or religion. They have been victims of abuse, molestation, violence, rape, poverty, malnutrition, ill treatment in a world all sorts of deprivation. But until recently, scholarly attention was not focused enough on subjects related to empowerment of women. In the multi-cultural, multi-lingual, multi-racial and multi-religious Indian sub-continent, women face one or other kinds of problem here and there. Only the dimension differs from state to state, society to society, and place to place. Even in the 21st century women are beaten, considered witches; they are getting stoned for committing sexual activities; honor killing is in practice in many parts of India; and with petty excuses they are tortured and raped while the main perpetrators move freely without any punishment. Further, they are disallowed to use mobile phones; debarred to choose their own dress or profession; have little freedom in marriage and reproductive matters; are restrained to move freely within their locality;

are discouraged to participate in political activities; and many women remain starved or half fed.

In a word, they are bound in chains of societal taboos and face lots of peculiar difficulties throughout their life. It is a fact that women have been suffering in every age and country from their protectors i.e. fathers, brothers, uncles, neighbors and others in childhood; boyfriends and lovers in youth; husbands and in-laws in married life; while from sons and others in old age. Man has inflicted an unspeakable injury upon woman by subjugating her in different phases in their lives and through the ages. Thus this question of woman's rights was a world question, and as old as the human race. In all ages, woman has considered by men as inferior, and had robbed of the rights, with which God had endowed her, in common with every human being" (Langley & Fox, 1994)

Women are the victims of social, political, religious, and economic subordination and deprivation in Indian society. Also they are treated unequally and cannot participate in democratic activities equally with men. Democracy becomes meaningless and paralyzed unless fifty per cent of its population participates in the democratic decision making processes and joins in the economic, social, and political activities. Therefore, to make democracy sustainable it is necessary that both women and men should take part in the development activities. Without the active participation of fifty per cent population i.e., women, the development of India is sure to be partial. It can be said that, where few take part in decisions there is little democracy; the more participation there is in decisions, the more democracy there is (Verba&Nie, 1972).

Thus the issue of women's empowerment through participation in various developmental activities has become sine qua non.The terms include self-strength, self-control, self-power, self-reliance, personal choice, capability of fighting for one's rights, independence, own decision making power, freedom etc.These definitions are embedded in local value systems and beliefs. Empowerment has both intrinsic as well as instrumental value. "The most common use of the term "empowerment" refers to increasing the Power of the low-power group, so that it more nearly equals the power of the high power group" (Bhadra, 2001).

According to SushamaSahay (1998), Empowerment is an active, multi-dimensional process which enables women to realize their full identity and powers in all spheres of life. It implies decentralization of power and authority in the deprived, oppressed and powerless people who have not been able to participate in decision making and implementation of policies and programs of both governments' organizations as well as in societal matters. Empowerment of women is not only essential but also imperative for all round development of a country. The term empowerment has been defined as that, empowerment is multi-dimensional and refers to the expansion of freedom of choice and action in all spheres (social, economic, and political) to shape one's life. It also implies control over resources and decisions ArundhatiChattopadhyaya (2005).

Further the term empowerment is defined as the process of gaining control over one's own life while supporting and facilitating others' control over their lives (Aspy&Sandhan). Goodrich describes empowerment as "a benevolent but unilateral transaction in which one person enhances another's ability to feel competent and take action, that is, enhances another's power-to" (Patricia, Darlington & Mulvane, 2003).

The World Bank also defines the term empowerment as "the process of increasing the capacity of individuals or groups to make choices and to transform those choices into desired actions and outcomes.

Central to this process are actions which both build individual and collective assets and improve the efficiency and fairness of the organizational and institutional context which govern the use of these assets (Chattopadhyay, 2005).

As we know in democracy the voice of all is being heard equally. But, throughout history, women which constitute fifty percent of global populations are underrepresented indecision-making processes at all governance levels around the world and even they are dominated and marginalized politically, socially, economically, physically and psychologically by their counter parts. Therefore, the participation of women in the political discourse is a recent phenomenon. The participation of women in political decision-making positions was recognized as a political right after the adoption of the Universal Declaration of (UDHR) in 1948.UDHR Articles 2 and 21 stipulate equal enjoyment of political rights without discrimination on the basis of one's sex or any other ground. Even in most of western states women franchise right is not recognized in the first wave of democratization except in USA, Britain and some European countries.

1.3 The National Context,

Like many world countries, the majority of women in Ethiopia has also deprived of social, economic and political rights and hold low status in the society for much history of the country. They have been denied equal access to education, training and gainful employment opportunities and their involvement in policy formulation and decision-making processes have been minimal. Ethiopia has previously submitted periodic national reports on the implementation of the Beijing Declaration and Platform for Actionin1999, 2004, 2009 and 2014th at highlighted the progress and achievements recorded as well as the gap and limitations encountered. This fifth report is submitted on the 25 anniversary of the Beijing Declaration and Platform for Action to provide relevant information on progress made and challenges faced in the implementation of the BDPF a commitment during the five years period between 2014-2019 subsequent to the last report. This report was prepared through participatory process involving relevant government and non-government stakeholders at different levels. The report preparation process was led by the Ministry of Women, Children and Youth (MoWCY) with the support of a Steering Committee (comprised of State Ministers from relevant sector ministries) and a Technical Committee of experts under the auspices of the (MoWCY).

While Ethiopia has made significant strides over the recent years in setting the corner stone's of a women's machinery in government. The present government has given priority to the speeding up of equality between men and women. Practically for example the government formulated national policy on women in 1993 with the objective of speeding up of equality between men and women, so that women can participate in the political, social, and economic life of their country on equal terms with men, ensuring that their right to own property as well as other human rights are respected and that they are not excluded from the enjoyment of the fruits of their lab our or from performing public functions and being decision makers. Hence the article centers on two main substantive parts. The first part focuses on the factors that hinder women political participation in Ethiopia and secondly the importance of women political participation. The 1994 Education and Training Policy affirmed the importance of girls' education. It focused on the reorientation of the attitude and values of the society towards recognizing the roles and contributions of women in development. The policy included gender equality issues such as increasing girls' school enrolment ratio, preparing a gender sensitive curriculum, and reducing girls' dropout and repetition rates (FDRE, 1994).

1.4 Types of Empowerment

It is evident from the above discussions that different authors and organizations have tried to define the term 'empowerment' from their own perspectives. It ranges from self-strength to efficiency building of women. However, empowerment of women now can be categorized into five main parts social, educational, economic, political and psychological.

1.4.1 Social Empowerment

Social Empowerment refers to the enabling force that strengthens women's social relations and their position in social structures. Social empowerment addresses the social discriminations existing in the society based on disability, race, ethnicity, religion, or gender. Empowerment as a methodology is often associated with feminism. Broadly put, the term empowerment is defined as "a multi-dimensional social process that helps people gain control over their own lives. It is a process that fosters power in people for use in their own lives, their communities and in their society by acting on issues they define as important. A nearly similar definition has been given by Valsamma Antony (The Kurukshetra, February 2006). She considers that, empowerment of women is a multi-dimensional process, which should enable the individual's or group of individuals to realize their full identity and powers in all spheres of life. Empowerment of women means enjoyment of equal rights, equal status and freedom of self-development with men. Valsamma Antony quoted Mikhail Gorbachev, former President of the USSR, in one of her articles. Gorbachevopined that, "The status of women is a barometer of the democratic of any state, an indicator of how human rights are respected in it. From a sociological point of view, K.D. Gangrade (2001) has extended a definition of empowerment, considers women's empowerment as equal status to women opportunity and freedom to develop herself. Women are exploited in almost every society. Empowerment of women has been defined by Griffin (1987).

1.4.2 Educational Empowerment

"Traditional concepts recognize higher education as an instrument of personal development. It helps in growing an individual's intellectual horizons, wellbeing and potential for empowerment" (TheKurukshetra, September 2012). It is considered as the single most important instrument of socio-political and economic transformation. But the picture of women's educational empowerment is not rosy in India. "The recently released United Nations Development Report 2011 ranked India 134 out of 187countries (The Kurukshetra, September 2012). Without proper education to all children including girls, gender empowerment is not possible. This maxim if one male child is literate personally he alone becomes educated but if one girl child is educated the whole family becomes benefited - has been realized by the national political leaders, policy makers, administrators and bureaucrats. In this regard P.H. Sethumadhava Rao (2001) considers that, "The most important thing is that they (the women) need to be given free and compulsory education so as to make them aware of the rights and duties and possible free legal aid so that they can fight their cases without spending money." Education creates self-confidence, self-esteem, self-sufficiency to a person. It brings light of hope; increases social, political, intellectual, and cultural and religious consciousness; broadens the length of mind; removes all kinds of bigotry, narrowness, superstition and enhances fellow-feeling, tolerance etc.

Kiran Devendra (2001) stresses the importance of health, education and self-esteem of women. Devendra feels, "Empowerment of women would mean equipping women to be economically independent, self-reliant, have a positive self-esteem to enable them to face any difficult situation and they should be able to participate in developmental activities." Education plays a great role in this sphere. Women have to be empowered socially, educationally, politically, economically and culturally." He further states that, "When literacy percentage is increased, the women could be able to understand their actual rights which have been already given to them by the constitution of India and accordingly the provisions contained in Panchayati Raj itself Pathak (2003).

1.4.3 Economic Empowerment

Economic empowerment is the crying need of this hour. "Wage employment means economic power (Elliott, 2008). Through employment women earn money and it enables women and girls to become 'bread earners', contributing members of households with a strong sense of their own economic independence. "Economic empowerment is a powerful tool against poverty" (Biswas, 2010).

The Djakarta Declaration (1994) critically examines that, empowerment of women is not only equal consideration; it was a necessary precondition for sustainable economic and social development. Without economic self-sufficiency other rights and scopes remain meaningless to the people. Economic empowerment can be described as a means by which the poor, landless, deprived and oppressed people of all societies can be freed from all kinds of deprivation and oppression; can directly enjoy the benefits from markets as well as household; can easily manage a square nutritious food and fulfill basic requirements such as house, cloth, medicine and pure water etc. SEWA (Self Employed Women's Association) has emphasized on the economic empowerment of women. It holds that raising voice and visibility is not possible unless there is an access "to the ownership of economic resources by the poor women." PromillaKapur (2001) observes that, "women's empowerment could be described as a process in which women gain greater share of control over resources - material, human and intellectual like knowledge, information, ideas and financial resources like money and access to money and control over decision making in the home, community, society and nation, and to gain power. Economic empowerment gains through equal work opportunities, equal organizational benefits, equal treatments and equal working environment. Economic empowerment is also the empowering of previously disadvantaged sections of the population (Retrieved from http://en.wikipedia.org/wiki/Empowerment).

1.4.4 Political Empowerment

Participation of women in the political field and in various decision-making bodies is an important tool for empowerment. The participation of women at all levels of governance structures is the highest need of this hour for women's actual empowerment. Alida Brill (2000) holds that, "Without our own voices being heard inside the government areas and halls of public policy and debate, we are without the right to accountability a basic establishment of those who are governed. In other words, "Empowerment is not giving people power; people already have plenty of power, in the wealth of their knowledge and motivation, to do their jobs magnificently. We define empowerment as letting this power out (Blanchard, Carlos, Randolph, 1996). It encourages people to gain the skills and knowledge that will allow them to overcome obstacles in life or work environment and ultimately, help them develop within themselves or in the society.

Women throughout the world have been struggling to break away the shackle of bondage, Subjugation, oppression and all kinds of ill treatment both within and outside of their families. Without bringing them in the corridor of power where they can formulate policies and programs and implement them, the survival of women is very difficult. Pam Raj put (2001) also supports the view. According to Rajput, "Empowerment of women in all spheres, in particular the political sphere is crucial for their advancement and the foundation of a gender equal society. It is central to the achievement of the goals of equality, development and peace." Without political participation it would be very difficult for women to increase effectiveness, capacity, challenging the existing power structure and patriarchal ideology. Politics decide who will get what and how much. Hence, empowering women politically is the highest need of the hour. Women's political empowerment implies the decentralization of power and authority in the deprived, oppressed and powerless people who have not been able to participate in the decision making processes and implementation of policies and programs of both government organizations as well as familial and societal matters.

The feminist scholar and activist Srilatha Batliwala (1995) expresses her view of empowerment as the process of challenging existing power-relations, and of gaining greater control over the sources of power, may be termed as empowerment."

Kamala Bhasin (1998) also broadly defines the term empowerment. Bhasin cites that, "It means recognizing women's contribution, women's knowledge; it means helping women fight their own fears, and feeling of inadequacy and inferiority; it means women enhancing their self-respect and self-dignity; it means women controlling their own bodies; it means women becoming economically independent and self-reliant; it means women controlling resources like land and property; it means reducing women's burden of work, especially within the home; it means creating and strengthening women's groups and Organizations.

Prasad (2002) views that, Empowerment is a process geared towards participation, greater decision making and transformative action through awareness and capacity building". Empowerment can otherwise be cited as a multi process, which requires pooling of resources to gather power and strength. Since empowerment of women depends largely on their participation in social and political activities, it is necessary to understand the nature of political participation also. Various scholars have defined the term political participation in different ways. But there is a common thread that connects of them. It is closely related with power and it very much exists in democratic societies. Miller holds that, It is the activity which aims at bringing government to bear in a particular direction, to secure particular results (Carolyn, 2008). Lass well assume that, "Political process is the shaping, sharing and exercise of power. By joining politics people feel themselves empowered. It is a ladder for upward mobility in society. It is a route to empowerment for the deprived and the powerless. Through political participation, people find opportunities to change and influence public decisions and to bring them in their favor. They can also protect their self-interest and legitimate rights and promote justice for the common men (Niroj, 2000).

1.4.5 Psychological Empowerment

Through psychological empowerment, women can not only transgress the traditional and patriarchal taboos and social obligations, they also transform their selves and subjectivities. When women join educational institutions, political parties or decision-making bodies; take decisions and travel different places; occupy land and wealth they feel psychologically powered and build their self-confidence, recognize their self-worth and take control of their own income and body. This joining in any institution and occupation gives them opportunities to see and to know more of the world than those who have stayed behind at home. "This personal growth and exploration has given them self-respect, pride, maturity, and resiliency as they have exerted theirindependenceawayfromhome(http://www.joe.org/joe/1999october/comm1.php).

Status of Women

One of the areas of imbalance between males and females is related to the difference in their employment status which is manifested by occupational segregation, gender-based wage gaps, and women's disproportionate representation in informal employment, unpaid work and higher unemployment rates (UNFPA, 2005).

As women in developing countries have low status in the community, the activities they performed to be valued less and women's low status is also perpetuated through the low value placed on their activities (Marchet al., 1999).

In-depth analysis of DHS by Hind in (2005) showed that only 17% of women in Zimbabwe, 12% in Zambia and 4% in Malawi have higher status job than their partners. The respective percentages of women whose partners have higher status jobs are 52, 43 and 53.

Women are also overrepresented in the informal sector. In Sub-Saharan Africa, 84% of women are non-agricultural employment is informal compared to 63% of men's. The figure is found to be 58% and 48% for women and men, respectively in Latin America (UNFPA, 2005). Studies generally show that women are more likely to be engaged in work and also work for longer hours than men.

1.5 Statement of the Problem

Women's empowerment and economic development are closely related: development can play a major role in driving down inequality between men and women; in the other direction, empowering women also may benefit development (Duflo, 2012). Empowered women can influence the positive change in their household. Empowerment of women, when looking at their access to health, information and control of resources such as money, is important for achieving gender equality and health equity. However, the ratio of female-to-male earned income is below similarity in all countries for which data are available (WHO, 2013).Specifically, there is evidence that when transfer payments are given to women rather than to their husbands, expenditures on children go up for women than for men. This shows that women access to resources has a higher impact on spending on children which promotes human-capital accumulation; this recommends that empowering women may ultimately lead to faster economic growth (Doepke & Tertilt, 2011).

Different studies indicated that, the low status of women in developing countries in general and in Ethiopia in particular (Almaz, 1991; Hirut, 2004; Mukuria et al., 2005). Lack of access to productive resources such as land; lack of access to education, employment opportunities, basic health services, and protection of basic human rights; low decision making; violence and harmful traditional practices are some of the indicators of the socio-economic marginalization of women in the country. Such gender gap between men and women in socio-economic indicators has negative impact on the overall development of the country in general and on demographic and health outcomes of individuals in particular.

According to Kishor (2005), gender differences in power, roles and rights affect health, fertility control, survival and nutrition through women's access to health care, lower control over their bodies and sexuality, and restrictions in material and non-material resources.

The socialization process, which determines gender roles, is partly responsible for the subjugation of women in the country. Ethiopian society is socialized in such a way that girls are considered as a inferior to boys. In the process of upbringing, boys are expected to learn and become self-reliant, major bread winners, and responsible in different activities, while girls are brought up to conform, be obedient and dependent, and specialize in indoor activities like cooking, washing clothes, fetching water, caring for children, etc. (Haregewoin and Emebet, 2003; Hirut, 2004).

Women are still experiencing negative treatment from their family, community, administration and even from their similar sex partners (that is women). The problem is even worse in developing countries. Ethiopia is one of the developing countries where women are facing political, social and cultural challenges that undermine their human right and dignity. They are suffering from economic poverty, social discrimination, political disenfranchisement, and cultural subjugation (Helina, 2015; UN, 2014).

The focus of this study would be to discuss the practice and challenges of Government program toward women empowerment and its effect on the family as well as Society, specifically women and the researcher would examine the gender gap in some socio-economic and demographic profile indicators in the Makuey Woreda of Nuer Nation Zone. Like any other areas, Inequality is a major social problem in Makuey Woreda. The researcher would try to look at some cases in Makuey woreda. This research aims to explore the women viewpoints on the women empowerment in Ethiopia, the case of Makuey Woreda in Gambella region. It would also help to identify inequality faced by Women and how to dismantle those problems they face, the effect of this study would have both basic academic and applied practical purpose.

1.6 Objectives of the Research

1.6.1. General Objective

The general objective of this study was to identify the practices and challenges of Government Program toward women empowerment in Makuey woreda, Ethiopia.

1.6.2. Specific Objectives

The specific objectives of this research were:

- To identify the practice of Government program towards empowerment of Women in the study area.
- To identify the challenges of Government program towards women empowerment in the study area.
- To identify the effects of practices in Government program towards Women empowerment in Makuey Woreda.

- To identify the extent of gender gap in term of socio-economic and demographic profile indicators such as, educational attainment, employment, age at first marriages; i.e. to carry out gender analysis on available data.

1.7 Research Question

- What were the practices in Government program towards Women empowerment in the study area?
- What were the Challenges of Government program towards Women in the study area
- What were the effects of practices of Government program towards women empowerment in the study area?
- What was the extent of gender gaps in term of socio-economic and demographic profiles

1.8 Significance of the Study

The purpose of this study was to identify the practices and challenges of Government Program toward women empowerment and the effect of educational, psychological, political and socio-economic empowerment on women in Makuey Woreda, it has a number of significant for different organs, enabling the concerned body such as women and social affairs of the Woreda to take action to reduce the rate of inequality and its impact on the society as a whole and women in particular.

The outcomes of this study would be used as an input by the government to formulate the public policies and strategies at local and national levels to reduce the rate of discrimination and its impact on the society.

The finding of the study also would help the ministry of lab our and social affair at federal level and the respective regional office in designing social policy relating maintenance of society. This study would serve as an initiative and further reference for other researchers who need to conduct study on the empowerment on Vulnerable Group, particularly women.

It may serve as a reference material in the academic sphere.

It can provide valuable information about the practices and challenges of Government program towards women empowerment in Markey Woreda.

It can indicate possible solution of program that discriminated Women in makuey woreda.

It would change the policy that challenges and discriminate the right of Women in Makuey Woreda.

It may be useful with people who would practice the empowerment policy in Makuey Woreda.

1.9 Scope of the Study

This study would be conduct in Makuey Woreda, Ethiopia. It is found in Gambella regional state. The study was expected to be carried out according to the university schedule. In general, the scope of this study was limited to identify the practices and challenges of Government program toward the women empowerment in three government organization and two kebeles in Makuey Woreda. The successful of empowerment may be many in numbers and the researcher in this study was discussing the major one, mainly due to time and budget constrain. In the same fashion due to time and budget constraint the researcher would be limited this study to the education, psychological, political, and socio- economic women empowerment in Makuey Woreda, Ethiopia.

1.10 Delimitation of the Study

Any research undertaking would face certain limitations though the degree of challenge varies depending up on the nature and type of research problems and the study area. Accordingly, the following limitations of this study;

1. Might be shortage of time.
2. During conducting interview with key informant persons some of them might not be available on time for interview due different problems may they occupied by other job.

1.11 Organization of the Study

This study would be organized in five main parts. The first

chapter would be consists of the introduction part of the study which was the Research proposal. The introduction part deals with background, statement of the problem, research questions, objective of the study, significance of the study, delimitation. The second chapter would involved a brief review of related literature regarding the practices, the challenges and effect of Government program towards women empowerment on the whole society in general and women in particular. The third chapter would deals with research methods and methodology and description of the study area. Besides this, the fourth chapter would articulate data presentation and analysis of the study under different sections. Finally, the last chapter (five) would stipulate conclusion and recommendation.

Chapter Two

Literature Review

2.1 Concept or Definition of Women Empowerment

Several detailed reviews and papers have captured the debate on the meaning and measurement of empowerment. Depending on context and author, empowerment has been associated with a wide range of definitions. Terms that most often overlap across various definitions refer to choice, power, options, control, and agency. Women empowerment refers to increasing the spiritual, political, social, educational, gender or economic strength of individuals and communities of women. Women empowerment is believed to be an important factor in determining the utilization of child health practices. When women are empowered, children can lives comfortable, and the countries flourish reaping a double dividend for women and children" (Former UN secretary Kofi A. Annan).

The FAO estimates that women comprise approximately 43 percent of the agricultural labor force in developing countries (varying by country and by region) and, on average, have less access to and control over productive resources than men have (resources such as land, education, labor, livestock, technology, financial and extension services). The FAO has estimated that closing this asset gap could result in a yield increase on women's farms by 20 to 30 percent, raising agricultural output in developing countries by 2.5 to 4 percent and reducing the number of hungry people globally by 12 to 17 percent (FAO, 2011).

Empowerment is hence described as the expansion of agency but also the expansion of the "opportunity structure" (formal and informal institutional context in which people operate) and their interaction that is required before empowerment can take place (Alsop, Bertelsen, and Holland 2006; Alsop and Heinsohn 2005).

Women empowerment and development issues form the basis to achievement of sustainable development, peace and progress in both developed and developing countries. Empowerment of women, when looking at their access to health, information and control of resources such as money, is important for achieving gender equality and health equity. However, the ratio of female-to-male earned income is below similarity in all countries for which data are available (WHO, 2013).

Women's empowerment and gender equality concepts are important in fostering health and human development. Empowerment describes the process of change where an individual with prior inability to choose has the access and freedom to make choices (Kabeer, 2005).

2.2. The practices of Government Program towards Women empowerment

The work on women empowerment in the real sense started with the establishment of 'United Nations' after the second world war. In its charter on January 26, 1945, the equal rights for men and women were affirmed for the first time. The charter of the UNS is the first legal document pronouncing against discrimination to the basis of sex. The Economic and Social Council known as ECOSOC is the principal Organ of the UN to co-ordinate the economic and social work of the UN. The ECOSOC established the Commission on the Status of Women in June 1946. The two main functions of this commission were;

1. To prepare recommendations and report to Economic and social council on promoting women's rights in political, economic, civil, social and educational fields.
2. To make recommendations on urgent problems requiring immediate attention in the field of women's rights. The UNS

adopted CEDAW - The Convention for the Elimination of the Discrimination against Women in December 1979 to ensure equality of men and women in the exercise of human rights and fundamental freedoms in every field.

Historically, women have played significant socio-political and economic roles across the world, the experience in Africa, particularly in recent years attests to this conclusion Aside from the fact that the academia and international development institutions, through research, have documented the concrete contributions of women to Africa's development, their input into the socio-political and economic transformation of the continent has been globally appreciated (Bunch, Charlotte and Roxanna Carrillo, 1990).

African women also occupy strategic positions in international development institutions such as the World Bank (WB), the United Nations (UN), the International Monetary Fund (IMF) and other similar global institutions worldwide making impacts on global development From the colonial epoch to the present day post-cold war era, accounts of women's contributions to the development of a united Africa are aptly amplified as expected Politically, women participated actively in different colonial African states to liberate the countries from foreign domination Economically; they have contributed significantly to Africa's economic growth, particularly in areas such as agriculture, trade and commerce Socially.

The status of women in the Cameroonian society that was often dwarfed and subordinated to that of men by culture and state institutions is gradually being reversed with the adoption of the AU's Institutional and legal framework on In 2011, Alliances for Africa, an African-led human rights, peace and sustainable development NGO in Lagos, Nigeria collaborated with Unilever Nigeria, a manufacturer of personal products and consumer goods, to pilot a Women Empowerment Programme (WEP) over a 1-year period. This was an Economic Empowerment Scheme designed to contribute to Goals 1 and 3 of the Millennium Development Goals (MDGs) aimed at combating poverty and improving gender equality respectively. Important background facts; If men and women had equal access to productive resources in agriculture, food output in developing countries would increase by between 2 5 and four percent - enough topull100150million people out of hunger Yet women continue to be discriminated against in accessing these resources, (FAO 2011).

Ethiopia, in-order to eliminating gender gap (discrimination) and to enhance women's Participation in all spheres of life, formulated women's National Policy in 1993. National institutional machineries were established at federal, regional and Woreda (district) levels to implement the policy. The Women's Affairs Office has been reestablished as a full-fledged Ministry in October 2005 with the duties and responsibilities of ensuring participation and empowerment of women in political, economic, social and cultural matters.

The Women's Policy primarily aims to institutionalize the political, economic, and social rights of women by creating an appropriate structure in government to offices and institutions so that the public policies and interventions are gender-sensitive and can ensure equitable development for all Ethiopian men and women. Article 25 of Ethiopian constitution put that all persons are equal before the law and are entitled without any discrimination to the equal protection of the law. In addition to this the constitution provides women with general protection from male domination and equality in terms of various engagements. Article 34(1) of Ethiopian constitution reads as men and women, without any distinction as to race, nation, nationality or religion, who have attained marriageable age as defined by law, have the right to marry and found a family.

The Ethiopia National Policy on Women (Women's Policy) formulated in 1993, aimed to create appropriate structures within government offices and institutions to establish equitable and gender-sensitive public policies. The Government of Ethiopia in 1995, under its new constitution, renewed its commitment towards this policy. The government initiated an ambitious and extensive process of regionalization, whereby new regional boundaries were demarcated and administrative powers devolved to regional governments, which were authorized to implement all development policies. This represented a departure from the earlier practice of centralized project management by ministries FDRE 1993.

The issue of gender equality has become an area of concern in development planning during the last few decades. The marginalization, from development programs, of women for a long period of time is challenged with changing policy perspectives from Women in Development (WID), which aims to include women in development projects in order to make the latter more effective, to Gender and Development (GAD), which aims to address inequalities in women's and men's social roles in relation to development . Gender mainstreaming, the integration of gender issues into every aspect of development programs, is aimed at empowering women to enable them participate in and benefit from the programs equally as men, being supported by international and national policies (March et al., 1999).

This more participatory and decentralized form of governance made the implementation of the national policy a more challenging endeavor. There was correspondingly a great need to build the delivery capacity of the regional governments. While the central level of government promoted gender-sensitive policies and development interventions, very little was known about the constraints and issues at the regional levels. Objectives of the Women in Development (WID) Report Discussions with the Minister, Women's Affairs Office initiated the process of preparing a report with a regional focus. The procedure for preparation was discussed with the government and other relevant stakeholders. Issues were identified jointly through Participatory Rural Appraisals (PRA) to bring in the voices of grassroots women stakeholders and through preparation of background reports by a number of local consultants. The WID report examines and identifies institutional, legal, and regulatory constraints on the expeditious and effective implementation of the women's policy. The success in achieving gender parity at primary level is anchored on the well-articulated and envisioned mission of the Education Sector Development Program (ESDP I-IV) of the country. The problems of gender inequalities are very much prevalent in and relevant to Ethiopia. Ethiopia is a patriarchal society that keeps women in a subordinate position (Haregewoin and Emebet, 2003).

There is a belief that women are docile, submissive, patient, and tolerant of monotonous work and violence, for which culture is used as a justification (Hirut, 2004).The socialization process, which determines gender roles, is partly responsible for the subjugation of women in the country. Ethiopian society is socialized in such a way that girls are held inferior to boys. In the process of upbringing, boys are expected to learn and become self-reliant, major bread winners, and responsible in different activities, while girls are brought up to conform, be obedient and dependent, and specialize in indoor activities like cooking, washing clothes, fetching water, caring for children, etc (Haregewoin and Emebet, 2003; Hirut, 2004).

The differences in the ways in which individuals are treated through the socialization process, due mainly to their sex status, leads to the development of real psychological and personality differences between males and females (Almaz, 1991). For instance, a female informant in Arsi stated that a man is a big person who has higher social position and knowledge, who can govern others and think in wider perspectives; while a woman is a person who can serve a man, who is like the husband's object transferred through marriage, and to whom he can do anything he wishes to do (Hirut, 2004).

These socially induced differences between males and females result in discriminatory rewards, statuses, opportunities and roles as shall be discussed below. Low educational level is one of the causes and consequences of females' low socio-economic status. In spite of the fact that significant progress has been realized in girls' education during the last decade, gender gap is still observed. According to various statistical abstracts of the Ministry of Education, the share of female students has increased from 21% to 25% between the years 1998/99 and 2002/03. Nevertheless, the sex disaggregated Gross Enrolment Ratio (GER), the ratio of total enrolment at primary or secondary education to the corresponding school age population, shows disparity between the two sexes. Though female GER in primary education has increased from 41% in 1999/2000 to 54% in 2002/03, the respective figures for males are 61% and 75%. The gender gap is clearly observed when the Gender Parity Index (GPI), the ratio of female to male enrolment, is considered. Between the years 1999 and 2003, GPI was found to be 0.7, indicating that there were only 7 girls enrolled at primary schools for every 10 boys (Federal Civil Service Commission, 2005).

The breakdown of the federal government employees by occupational groups also indicated gender disparity. From federal government employees found in the clerical and fiscal type of jobs 71.3 % were female, while the percentage of females was slightly more than half (51%) in custodial and manual type of jobs. Women make up 25% and 18% of the administrative, professional, and scientific job categories, respectively, indicating that men (Federal Civil Service Commission, 2005) overwhelmingly dominate upper and middle level positions. This concentration of women in the informal sector and low-level positions has implication on their earnings. In this regard, the survey showed four out of ten women civil servants earn Birr 300 a month compared to two out of ten for men (Federal Civil Service Commission, 2005).

Though women in the country have constitutional rights of participation in decision-making, their involvement is limited at all levels. Some of the Determinants of Women empowerment;

2.2.1. Women empowerment through education

Information Technology and media (both electronic and print) are assuming pivotal roles in dissemination of knowledge to the people and bringing the world nearer to one's reach. In the present day situation it is not possible for any society to think about empowerment without the incorporation and utilization of IT. The empowerment process is one where women find time and space of their own, and begin to re-examine their lives critically and collectively. Women's empowerment is a state of being that reflects a certain level of critical consciousness about external realities and an awareness about their internal thought construction and belief systems that affect their well being in terms of gender justice and social justice; as well as the determination to use their physical, intellectual, emotional and spiritual resources to protect their lives and sustain values that guarantee gender equality and personal, social, economic, political and institutional level (Yojana, February 2003). Empowerment means freedom from deprivation; empowerment means equal access to knowledge and information; knowledge of being within groups of their own, empowerment also means organization; it means creation of information system and knowledge base Mukhopadhyaya (2003).

The 1994 Education and Training Policy affirmed the importance of girls' education. It focused on the reorientation of the attitude and values of the society towards recognizing the roles and contributions of Women in development. The policy included gender equality issues such as increasing girls' school enrolment ratio, preparing a gender sensitive curriculum, and reducing girls' dropout and repetition rates (FDRE, 1994).

In an attempt to address customary practices and backward traditions that undermine the roles of women in society, the National Cultural Policy was enacted in 1997. The main objectives of this policy are to ensure equal participation in and benefit from cultural activities, and to abolish traditional harmful practices that violate the rights of women such as early marriage, female genital mutilation and abduction (FDRE, 1997).

Despite the fact that the country adopted global agreements and endorsed country-specific laws and policies, there are gaps and limitations in implementation, as a result of which the status of women in the country remained very low as discussed in the first part. It is imperative, therefore, to revisit policy implementation strategies and programs, identify problem areas and take appropriate action for improvement. There is a direct co-relation between women's education and women empowerment. Literacy and education is the gateway to achieve women empowerment because the denial of access to education is the denial of access to status and power. Keeping women ignorant and unaware is to keep them disempowered and subordinate. Education empowers women is to take control of their lives. It increases the economic, social and political opportunities available to them.

It is the key to overcome oppressive customs and tradition. The Gender Gap was addressed through targeted measures that were taken to improve girls' access to primary education. These include: awareness raising programs on the importance of girls education; schools were made to be girls' friendly through the construction of separate latrines for girls and the assignment of female teachers and heads to provide close support to girls; rolling out of girls' clubs in schools as well as provision of tutorial, guidance and counseling services targeting female students. In Article 35, equality in matters related to employment, equality in acquisition and management of property, equal participation in policy and decision making, and right of women to plan families are stated to ensure gender equality. Similarly, Article 42 states the right of female Workers to equal pay for comparable work (FDRE, 1995).

2.2.2. Women Empowerment through Economic Activities

According to Tiwari (2001) examines the issue of women's empowerment in the context of Indian society and feminist women's liberation approach in the present-day environment. He has stated a few measures for women's empowerment which primarily focus attention on rejecting all restrictions, controls, limitations, values etc, on the ground that these are imposed on women only by patriarchy and are the revelation of male dominance But Kumud Sharma (1991-92) has rightly pointed out that "the term empowerment refers to range of activities from individual self-assertion to collective resistance, protest and mobilization that challenge basic power relations.

The Country Report of Fourth World Conference on Women in Beijing (1995) envisages that empowerment means changing from a position of enforced voiceless to one of power. It would promote women inherent strength and positive self-image. BidyutMohanty (1999) feels that the enactment of 73rd and 74th Constitution (Amendment) Acts needs citation is meant for women empowerment. Mohanty holds that, "the idea was to facilitate women's participation in grassroots politics, thereby empowering them to become partners in the decision-making process." ShakuntalaNarasimhan (1999) expresses her opinion in regard to women political empowerment. She opines that the word empowerment means Bringing women into the main-stream of national activity as equal partners alongside men.

The feminist scholar and activist SrilathaBatliwala (1995) expresses her view of empowerment as the process of challenging existing power-relations, and of gaining greater control over the sources of power, may be termed as empowerment. According to Chandra (1997), Empowerment in its simplest form means the manifestation or re-distribution of power that challenges patriarchal ideology and the male` domination." Mahatma Gandhi also spoke in favor of women's empowerment. He declares that," according to me empowerment may mean equal status to women, opportunity and freedom to develop herself (Gangrade, 2001).

Kamala Bhasin (1998) also broadly defines the term empowerment. Bhasin cites that, "It means recognizing women's contribution, women's knowledge; it means helping women fight their own fears, and feeling of inadequacy and inferiority; it means women enhancing their self-respect and self-dignity; it means women controlling their own bodies; it means women becoming economically independent and self-reliant; it means women controlling resources like land and property; it means reducing women burden of work, especially within the home; it means creating and strengthening women's groups and organizations; it means promoting qualities of nurturing, caring, gentleness not just in women but also in men." Women's empowerment is closely related with welfare and their development.

Nobel laureate Amartya Sen. Equates development with freedom, which he thinks, empowers women. The backwardness of a particular segment of society i.e., women, is mainly due to their failure to take part in development activities; though the failure is caused mainly by the obstructions put up by the patriarchal society. Also it is equally true that 'no one can empower any one.' Real empowerment is possible only by one's own effort. Empowerment is a process and is not, therefore, something that can be given to people the process of empowerment is both individual and collective, since it is through involvement in groups that people most often begin to develop their awareness and the ability to organize to take action and to bring about change" (Karl, 2002).

Prasad (2002) views that, empowerment is a process geared towards participation, greater decision making and transformative action through awareness and capacity building". Empowerment can otherwise be cited as a multi-process, which requires pooling of resources to gather power and strength. Since empowerment of women depends largely on their participation in social and political activities, it is necessary to understand the nature of political participation also. Various scholars have defined the term political participation in different ways. But there is a common thread that connects of them. It is closely related with power and it very much exists in democratic societies. Miller holds that, "It is the activity which aims at bringing government to bear in a particular direction, to secure particular results" (Carolyn, 2008).

Lass well assume that, "Political process is the shaping, sharing and exercise of power" (Niroj, 2000).By joining politics people feel themselves empowered. It is a ladder for upward mobility in society. It is a route to empowerment for the deprived and the powerless. Through political participation, people find opportunities to change and influence public decisions and to bring them in their favor. They can also protect their self-interest and legitimate rights and promote justice for the common men. Traditionally the concept of politics is related to government structures. But currently the notion of politics is taking a new and different shape. Movements, strikes, protests, demonstrations, struggles, processions etc. have become the legitimate expression of political engagement. Political participation and shouting slogans have grown as the language of influencing and bargaining different decisions and policies of different government and non-government organizations in favor of its participants. But is should be remembered that empowerment of women would never mean the acquirement of power and authority by the women to subjugate and dominate their opposite sex or to one group of women by another. That is not desired at all. Women's empowerment means to distribute equal power and authority between men and women and creating an environment of freedom from domination and suppression. The empowerment of women concerns women gaining control and power over their own lives. It involves awareness raising, building self-confidence, and expansion of choices, increased access to and control over resources (Yojana, March 2003).

The first is equity as valuable in and of itself: women are currently worse-off than men, and this inequality between genders is repulsive in its own right. For example, in the Millennium Development Goals (MDG), Kofi Annan, the Secretary General of the United Nations, writes: The full participation of women to all levels of decision-making is a basic human right. The second, a central argument in the discourse of policymakers, is that women play a fundamental role in development. The gender gap in education, political participation, and employment opportunities should therefore be reduced not only because it is equitable to do so, but also because it will have beneficial consequences on many other society-wide outcomes. It should be done, in other words, to increase efficiency. Accordingly, in the same report, Kofi Annan argues that gender equality is in fact a "prerequisite" to achieving the other MDGs.The stance that women empowerment is desirable for efficiency shapes both the policy debate and the resultant economic policies the world over. Micro-credit schemes, for example, have been directed almost exclusively at women, because, it is argued, women invest the money in goods and services that improve the well-being of families, in goods that are conducive to development (United Nation's 2005 report).

2.2.3. Women Empowerment through Social Activities

Social sector include health care, education, childcare, water and sanitation, housing and other social needs. Proper attention to these factors from women's perspective, add to the well-being of women. Health is another important factor for achieving total development of human beings. According to the World Health Organization (WHO) a positive health status is defined as "a state of complete physical, mental and social well-being and not merely the absence of disease or infirmity (Kurukshetra, 2002).

Mira Shiva (2001) feels, "Women's empowerment means that women no matter where they are healthy, have enough for their needs, their own survival and that of their family and community, to be able to live with dignity, live and work in safe and caring environment, which allows their growth and holistic development i.e., physically, emotionally, socially, economically."Legal experts and lawyers have viewed and analyzed women's empowerment from their own perspectives. The preamble to the Charter of the United Nations emphasizes upon the member states "to reaffirm faith in fundamental human rights, in the dignity and worth of the human person, in the equal rights of men and women" (Levin, Leah, 2002).

Sujata Manohar (2001) defines women's empowerment in this respect. She envisages that, the key to women's empowerment is recognition and enforcement of women's human rights. In the light of 'equality before the law' and 'equal protection of the law,' the legal experts want to bring down all kinds of legal discrimination against women. Without the establishment of women's legal rights and human social order women's real empowerment will be far dream. Empowerment of women has been defined as being able to make a contribution at all levels of society and not just in the home Griffin (1987).

Empowerment is the process by which people, organization, or groups who are powerless or marginalized become aware of the power change at work in their life context, develop the skills and capacity for gaining some reasonable control over their lives, which they exercise, without ignore the rights of others and which coincides with actively supporting the empowerment of others in their community McWhirter (1994).

2.2.4. Women Empowerment through Political Rights and Provisions

Until gender parity is reached in government, women cannot reach complete equality with men in any sphere. The unequal participation of women in power and decision- making structures at the local, regional, national and international levels reflects structural, attitudinal and cultural barriers prevailing in all societies. Stereotyped gender roles remain a major obstacle in women's political empowerment. On one hand women are considered unfit for leadership; as a result of which political parties are hesitant to select women candidates from 'winnable seats' and on the other hand they have been restricted in the household responsibilities. That is why they could not enter in the political field. For actively involving women in defining the political, economic and social agenda and enhancing the performance and political skills of those women who are already at decision making positions, government should enhance formal and informal training facilities for them; which could impart to women the art of lobbying, raising funds, networking as well as campaigning. The Ethiopia National Policy on Women, introduced in 1993, was the first policy that is specifically related to the affairs of women The objectives of the policy include facilitating conditions conducive to the speeding up of equality between men and women so that women can participate in the political, economic and social life of their country on equal terms with men; ensuring that their right to own property as well as their other human rights are respected and that they are not excluded from both the enjoyment of the fruits of their lab our or performing public functions and participating in decision making(Jelaludin et al., 2001).

2.2.5 Psychological Empowerment

Through psychological empowerment women not only transgress

the traditional and patriarchal taboos and social obligations; they also transform their selves and subjectivities. When women join educational institutions, political parties or decision-making bodies; hold white color jobs, take decisions and travel different places; occupy land and wealth they feel psychologically powered and build their self confidence, recognize their self-worth and take control of their own income and body. This joining in any institution and occupation gives them opportunities to see and to know more of the world than those who have stayed behind at home. This personal growth and exploration has given them self-respect, pride, maturity, and resiliency as they have exertedtheirindependenceawayfromhome (http://www.joe.org/joe/1999october/comm1.php).

2.3 The Challenges of government Program towards Women Empowerment

Adapting domesticating several International and Regional conventions and declarations designed to ensure gender equality, recognizing the equality of male and female citizens by the Constitution of the FDRE and other laws and adopting several policies designed to narrow down gender gaps were meant to transform the deep rooted gender based discriminatory beliefs, values and practices in Ethiopia. To some extent, this has yielded results. For example, in the last two decades, we have seen some progress on females' participation in politics and education. There has also been a struggle in minimizing harmful practices such as early marriage; genital mutilation and dissemination against female on the issue of land and other property ownership as well as sending children to school, etc. Women's' participation in the public services (including on higher education institutions), the defenses and police, and in the economy too have been fairly increasing.

Nevertheless, there is still need for further transforming discriminatory attitudes towards the female gender at the workplace, in the public sphere and at home. The traditional patriarchy of Ethiopia which remains buttressed by religion and culture, which has been causing gender differentials in access, participation, and service provision across the education, health, economic systems and sectors still remain prevalent. Moreover, although the Ethiopian government has made large strides in setting the corner stone of institutional machinery at Federal, Regional and sub-regional levels, these institutions have limited capacity in reaching out the pre-dominantly agrarian and pastoralist society of Ethiopia, where gender based problems and gander disparity are highly pervasive.

The MoWYCA still have insufficient capacity to enforce changes towards gender sensitive intervention among other lines of Ministers and Regional bureaus, despite the WADs and WAB are in place. There is lack of strong coordinating mechanism among the institutions introduced to promote gender equality and empower women with stakeholders and partners working on the sector which results in duplications of efforts and resources. Due to capacity related and other problems, national policies and legal instruments, continental and local protocols, conventions and declaration adopted to ensure gender equality and the human rights of the citizenry have not been fully and strictly implemented [69].

As far as primary school level is considered, the proportion of females attending primary school in developing countries in general and in Sub-Saharan African (SSA) countries in particular is found to be limited compared to that of males. Therefore, among females of primary school age, only 17% of them in Niger (in 1998) and 21% of them in Burkina Faso (in 1998/99) were attending school, while the respective figures for males are 24% and 29% (Mukuria et al., 2005).

Given the provisions in constitution of federal republic of Ethiopia, personal observation shows that women's right is not protected as it was spelt in constitution and other legal and policy provisions. This is in tern because of the dominant role of government in the implementation of these provisions while undermining the role of other NGOs and community based organizations. Moreover, absence of vibrant women's organizations and women's networks partly challenging the implementation of constitutional provisions. The constitution indeed is also limited in certain aspects by taking article 34 (5) of the constitution, which empower customary law in resolving family issues, is still fraught with limitations. "For instance, it overly empowers religious and customary laws as arbiters of family matters such as divorce and inheritance. To quote the constitution article 34 (5) put that "This Constitution shall not preclude the adjudication of disputes relating to personal and family laws in accordance with religious or customary laws, with the consent of the parties to the dispute. Particulars shall be determined by law (Helina, 2015).

This in turn challenging gender equality and adversely affecting the interest and right of women as it tends to be patriarchal in nature. This leads not only to the deprivation of women from ownership of and decision making on valuable economic and natural resource but also violation of basic human right of women (FDRE, 1995).

2.4. The effect of practices in Government program towards women empowerment.

Education for girls has important effect on every dimension of development: lower child and maternal mortality rates; increased education attainment by daughter and sons; higher productivity; and improved environmental management. Together, these can mean faster economic growth and equally important, wider distribution of the fruits of growth. More education for girls will also enable more and more women to attain leadership positions at all levels of society. Autonomy or empowerment of women has been found to have a strong relationship with their health seeking behavior (Woldemicael G, 2010).

There is now a growing interest among researchers and policy makers to fully understand the impact and path (direct) ways of influence of women's autonomy (freedom of self action) and empowerment on reproductive health, particularly on use of family planning and unmet needs for contraception(the use of artificial methods to prevent pregnancy). Women's autonomy is also closely associated with the Millennium Development Goals (MDGs) related to gender equality, maternal health, and the newly added target on universal access to reproductive health. With the deadline to achieving the (MDGs) fast approaching, more and more governments and development partners are focusing on finding the best and cost effective ways to meet these and related targets affecting the Wellbeing of women and their families. Since the time attention has been drawn on women's autonomy and empowerment, researchers have defined this attribute as women's ability to make choices and execute the same in a specific situation. The United Nations Development Fund for Women (UNIFEM) has defined women empowerment as having access to and control over the means to make a living on a sustainable and long term basis, and receiving the material benefits of this access and control (Carr, 2000).

This definition is however limited in its scope of covering other dimensions of women's empowerment. Women's empowerment has also been defined as the enhancement of assets and capabilities of diverse individuals and groups to engage, influence and hold accountable the institutions which affect them (Bennett, 2002).

2.5. The extent of gender gaps in term of socio-economic and demographic profiles

Gender can be defined as a set of characteristics, roles, and behavior patterns that distinguish women from Men socially and culturally and relations of power between them (Women Information Centre, 2005). These Characteristics, roles, behavior patterns and power relations are dynamic; they vary over time and between different cultural groups because of the constant shifting and variation of cultural and subjective meanings of gender .The difference in power relations between men and women results in different gender roles, social roles and socially appropriate characteristics and behaviors (Hirut, 2004).

Gender gap in access to education is more pronounced at secondary and higher levels in SSA and Southern and Western Asia. According to UNFPA (2005), based on the 2001/02 millennium indicators data base of the United Nations, the ratio of females per 100 boys enrolled in secondary education was 46 in Benin, 57 in Equatorial Guinea, 60 in Cambodia, 62 in Djibouti and 65 in Burkina Faso. Generally, the report shows that, in most developing countries, gender disparities in access to education increase with increasing level of education. Among 65 developing countries for which the required data were available, about half have achieved gender parity in primary education, 20% of them achieved gender parity in secondary education, and only 8% of them in higher education (UNFPA, 2005).

One of the areas of disparity between males and females is related to the difference in their employment status which is manifested by occupational segregation, gender-based wage gaps, and women's disproportionate representation in informal employment, unpaid work and higher unemployment rates (UNFPA, 2005). As women in developing countries have low status in the community, the activities they perform tend to be valued less; and women's low status is also perpetuated through the low value placed on their activities (March et al., 1999). In-depth analysis of DHS by Hindin (2005) showed that only 17% of women in Zimbabwe, 12% in Zambia and 4% in Malawi have higher status job than their partners. The respective percentages of women whose partners have higher status jobs are 52, 43 and 53.Women are also overrepresented in the informal sector. In Sub-Saharan Africa, 84% of women's non-agricultural employment is informal compared to 63% of men's. The figure is found to be 58% and 48% for women and men, respectively in Latin America (UNFPA, 2005).

Action refers to sexual division of lab our. Actions are generally categorized into three: productive, reproductive, and community activities. Productive activities are those accomplished for income generation through Production of goods and services. Reproductive activities include child bearing and nursing, as well as activities performed for maintenance of the family, such as fetching water, cooking, collecting firewood, etc.

When the community activities are those performed for the welfare of the general community, such as attending meetings. In most cultures, reproductive activities are defined to be roles of women, whereas men heavily dominate productive and community activities. Focus shows the environment in which men and women operate. It is important in identifying gender gaps, particularly working at home or away from home. Gender 10 In-depth Analysis of the Ethiopian Demographic and Health Survey 2005stereotyping, and thereby gender inequality - the inequality of opportunity, right, responsibility, role, and access to and control over resources - is the result of socialization; gender roles are not necessarily determined by sex status. Socialization is defined as the process by which individuals acquire knowledge, skills and dispositions that enable them to participate as more or less effective members of a group and the society (Almaz, 1991:2). The socially constructed division of lab our results in different rewards, statuses, opportunities and roles (Hirut, 2004).

Different studies indicated the low status of women in developing countries in general and in Ethiopia in particular. Lack of access to productive resources such as land; lack of access to education, employment opportunities, basic health services, and protection of basic human rights; low decision making; violence and harmful traditional practices are some of the indicators of the socioeconomic marginalization of women in the country. Such gender gap between men and women in socio-economic indicators has negative impact on the overall development of the country in general and on demographic and health outcomes of individuals in particular (Almaz, 1991; Hirut, 2004; Mukuria et al., 2005).

Gender differences in power, roles and rights affect health, fertility control, survival and nutrition through women's access to health care, lower control over their bodies and sexuality, and restrictions in material and non-material resources. The process of correcting gender disparity in a society leads us to improving the condition and status of women in all spheres (household as well as community level) which is also termed as women's empowerment. It is a multi-dimensional concept, which purports to measure a woman's ability to control resources, her ability to choose and control different outcomes, and above all to enhance her self-esteem. It can be examined based on different indicators (Kishor, 2005).

These direct measures consist of a combination of observable items or indicators that are categorized into different dimensions of autonomy, such as access to and control over resources participation economic and child-related decisions, self-esteem, mobility, freedom from domestic violence, and political awareness and participation (Balk, 1994, 1997; Blumberg, 1994; Morgan and Niraula, 1995; Hashemi, Schuler and Riley, 1996; Jejeebhoy, 2000; Jejeebhoy and Sathar, 2001).

This variable is increasingly used as an objective indicator of women's household level empowerment, particularly in demographic and health studies (Schuler and Hashemi, 1994; Balk, 1997; Hindin, 2000; Kritz et al., 2000).

These problems of gender inequality are social problem in Ethiopia particularly in Makuey Woreda, so this study will be very important to identify and to remove these barriers and will enable other researchers to conduct research in the study area.

2.6 Conceptual Frame Work

This conceptual frame work focus on dependents and independent variable such as Educational empowerment, Political empowerment, and Economical empowerment and others

Picture 1: The conceptual frame works of the study to the women empowerment are as the following;

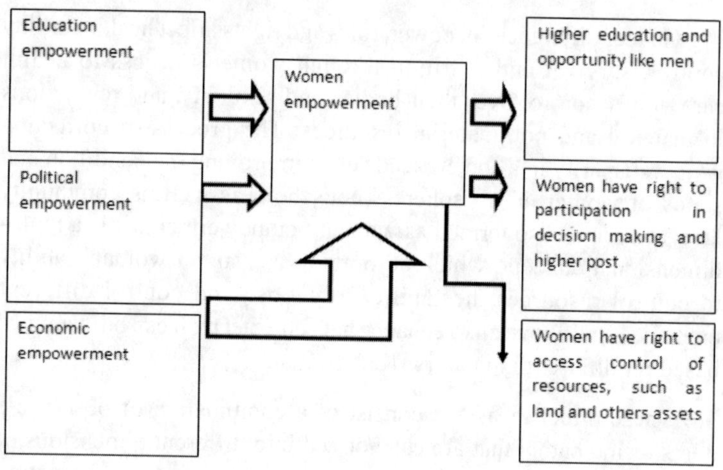

Source: adapted from Mukhopadhyaya (2003), (Elliott, 2008).

Chapter Three

Research Methodology

3.1 The description of study Area.

This study would be conducted in Makuey Woreda Nuer Nation Zone in Gambella regional state, Makuey is far from Addis Ababa at 853 km and 87 km from Gambella Regional State and it is found in Southern part of the region and Zonal town. The woreda bound with Itange special Woreda North side, North east with Lare Woreda, east with Jore woreda and South with Wanthoa woreda and west with Jekow Woreda. The Woreda have twenty one kebeles and has total population of 25352 peoples. The participants or stakeholders would be three governmental Offices and community from two kebeles including women by themselves. The governmental Institution that the survey would be among includes: the Women and Children Affair Office (WCAO) in the Makuey Woreda which is responsible to handle all social affairs' matters including empowerment, Makuey Woreda Education Office (MWEO), Makuey Woreda administration Office. This study would also include 01 and 02 kebele community members including Women to better understand how the community members treat those segments of vulnerable group.

3.2 Research Design

Research design is the overall plan for collecting data in order to answer the research question and also the specific data analysis techniques or methods that the researcher would intend to uses. This research would employ both qualitative and quantitative (mixed) approaches to identify an accurate description of the practices and challenges of Government program towards women empowerment in makuey woreda, Ethiopia.

3.2.1Quantitative Approaches

The quantitative approaches of this study would be used through survey method to collect data. The researcher would read difference documents from selected Organizations such as annual report and other. As it would includes both quantitative and qualitative research method to better understand the situation of empowerment of Women in Makuey Woreda, the quantitative design would be employed to survey and describe the general trend of organizations participant and serving of the community and women in particular.

3.2.2 Qualitative Approaches

A qualitative approach would be used to fully understand and describe the situation faced by these people discriminated by themselves, organizational staffs and direct protection providers or agency responsible to promote empowerment to these vulnerable people in the community. The researcher would go directly to observe how this vulnerable group is treated.

3.3 Data Sources and Sampling Technique

3.3.1 Sources of Data Collection

There are two sources of data collection, primary and secondary sources of data.

3.3.1.1 Primary Source of Data

The primary sources of data will be collected through the administration of questionnaires, interview, FGD, Field Observation from respondents.

3.3.1.2 Secondary Source of Data

Secondary sources of data would be obtained from annual report of selected Organizations of Makuey Woreda, women and Children affairs office, Educational office and Woreda Administration Office and from the report of selected two kebeles.

3.4 Methods of Data Collection

3.4.1 Field Observation and Informal Interviews

To identify the social, educational, psychological and economic empowerment of women in the selected Organization and kebeles, the researcher would observes those affected women. Direct personal observation would be made to the Institution and kebeles 'where the women are victim of inequality. Therefore, the researcher will go personally and observes the practices and challenges of Government program towards women empowerment in the selected Organization and kebeles' of makuey woreda and informal interview would be carried out with the victim.

3.4.2. Semi-Structured Questionnaires

Structured and unstructured survey questionnaire would be the main instruments of data collection for this study. The questionnaires would be distributed to 274 respondents and women in particular in the selected Institution and kebeles of the Woreda to investigate the practices and challenges of empowerment. To investigate the degree of prevalence of empowerment in the woreda, questionnaires will be distributed to employees of the Woreda education office, Woreda Administration, and women and children affair of the Woreda and Residents from selected of two kebeles.

3.4.3. Key Informant in Depth Interview

Another method of data collection for this study would be the in-depth interview with key informant persons that would be selected purposefully to gather detailed information that could not be acquired through questionnaire survey. To this end, semi-structured interview checklists would be developed as a guideline to raise questions. The member of key informant for this study would be the women and children affairs office head, educational office head and their employees of the organization and also would include two selected kebeles head. These key informant is selected because the researcher believe that they are the more concerned body with issue and have access to the practices and challenges of Government program towards women empowerment.

3.5. Sampling Techniques

The sampling design for this study would be both probability and non-probability sampling techniques. To select sample Organization and kebeles in the makuey woreda. Then, the members of key informant persons for interview would be selected by using snow ball technique. With snowballing, one information rich participant is identified and requested to identify others to take part in the study. On the other hands, the members of questionnaire respondent from the selected institution and kebeles of the makuey woreda would be selected randomly.

3.5.1 Sampling size

This study would employ Availability Sampling to include the Women by themselves to be the participant on the survey in order to convey the situation they face in the community and it would also apply purposive sampling such as Institutional staffs, and those are at higher managerial position that coordinate and are professional to deliver the support to the women in the study area. The target population for this study would be the three Government offices and Residents of two kebeles in makuey woreda.

According to Yemane (1976) as cited in (George, 2016), Since the target population, N, is known, the study used Yamane, Taro (1967) equation to calculate the sample size, n of the study population, N and e is the probability of error (within the desired precision of 0.05 for confidence level of 95 per cent).

$$n = \frac{N}{1+NE^2}$$

Whereas the

n = sample size

N = the size of the population

e = the margin of error

The sample size is calculated as follows based on this formula.

$$n = \frac{871}{1+871\times(0.05)^2}$$

$$n = \frac{871}{1+871(0.0025)}$$

$$n = 274$$

Therefore, sample size of the study would be 274. A total number of 274 People would participate in this study and they would be selected from three different respective Offices or institution and two kebeles as shown below the table.

Table 1: List of Institutions or stakeholder with their number of Participants that would participate on survey in the Makuey Woreda

Sl. No	*Name of the Organization/ Institution*	*Target population*	*No of Participants*
1.	01 and 02kebeles community (01 and 02 C) in Makuey Woreda	714	218
2.	Makuey Woreda Women and Children Office (MWCO)	29	12
3.	Makuey Woreda Education Office (MWEO)	80	29
4.	Makuey Woreda Administration Office (MWA)	48	15
	Total	871	274

3.6 Methods of Data Analysis

Both qualitative and quantitative methods of data analysis would be used in order to analyze the collected data. The findings of the study would be presented in tables, figures and charts. Some structured survey data would be analyzed using percentages, multiple response (frequency and cross tabulation), and descriptive statistics (frequency and cross tabulation) using the Statistical Package for Social Sciences (SPSS). On the other hands, discussions and interviews held with key informants persons would be also analyzed qualitatively. As such, qualitative data gathered from key informant interview and secondary sources would be analyzed by conceptual generalization and quantitative would be triangulated with qualitative data.

3.7 Ethical consideration

The researcher taken consideration in such a way that Informed consent of the participants is sought by explaining the purpose of the study and addressing any concerns like benefits, harmful effects and they are require to sign a consent form, and to ensure that the data is disclosed unreservedly, confidentiality of respondents would be assure as much as possible by avoiding identifiers like names, locations, and other forms of identification as well as Respecting their cultural beliefs, privacy of individual needs.

Chapter Four

Results and Discussions

This chapter deals with results and discussions of the data that are categorized into two parts. The first part treats the characteristics of the respondents which describe the study population by sex, age, education, experience, and marital status, while the second part deals with the analysis of findings of the study that were gathered through questionnaire, interview and observation.

In this study, both quantitative and qualitative methods of analysis were employed and the report was organized in a way to answer research questions raised in this research sequentially. Quantitative data which were collected through questionnaires and analyzed were supported and additionally evidenced by qualitative data which was collected from interviews.

4.1. Characteristic of respondents

As part of the general information, the respondents were requested to indicate their gender, age, marital status, level of education and years of service in their respective government public sectors. This was necessary in shedding light on the characteristics of the respondents.

Out of 274 respondents, 125(45.6%) were participated. From the sampling size 274, 37 (13.5%) of male and 21 (7.6%) of female were not turned back the document and the remaining respondents, 91(33.2 %) were not available. Among the respondents 83(66.4%) were male and 42(33.6) were female which indicated that the majority of the respondents were male.

4.1.1 Respondents' Gender

Inquiring about gender was necessary in determining whether there was gender balance in the government public sectors. The findings are contained in Table 2.

Table 2: Distribution of the respondents by Gender

Gender					
		Frequency	*Percent*	*Valid Percent*	*Cumulative Percent*
Valid	Male	83	66.4	66.4	66.4
	Female	42	33.6	33.6	100.0
				100.0	
Total		125	100.0		

Source: Field survey (2020)

According to the findings, 66.4 % of the respondents were male while 33.6% of the respondents were female. This was an indicated that there was gender disparity since the number of males exceeded that of females by far. This situation triggered the study to establish whether it would pose a challenge to women empowerment in the public sectors bureau.

4.1.2 Distribution of the respondents by age

Determining the respondents? age was important as it revealed their level of experience in dealing with the practices and challenges of women empowerment. Table 3 shows the age distribution of the respondents.

Table 3: Distribution of the respondent by age

Age					
		Frequency	*Percent*	*Valid Percent*	*Cumulative Percent*
Valid	below 21	7	5.6	5.6	5.6
	21-30	18	14.4	14.4	20.0
	31-40	79	63.2	63.2	83.2
	41-50	21	16.8	16.8	100.0
				100.0	
Total		125	100.0		

Source: Field survey (2020)

4.1.3 Distribution of the respondent by Educational level

Establishing the level of education helped in assessing how well the respondents understood and interpreted the questions. None of the respondents certificate level of education. The findings of this variable are shown in Table 4 that, those who has quality educational background can help their members to be a well participant for their business activities. As it was indicated from table 4 below

Educational level					
		Frequency	*Percent*	*Valid Percent*	*Cumulative Percent*
Valid	certificate	66	52.8	52.8	52.8
	Diploma	34	27.2	27.2	80.0
	degree	25	20.0	20.0	100.0
				100.0	
Total		125	100.0		

Source: Field survey (2020)

However, 52.8% of the respondents were certificate, 27.2% of the respondents were Diploma and 20.0% of the respondents were Bachelor Degree. Since majority of the respondents (52.8%) had Certificate qualifications, it was assumed that a large percentage of the respondents would be in a position to answer the questions appropriately.

4.1.4 Distribution of the respondent by experience

This question was expected to shade light on how experienced the respondents were in dealing with gender issues with regard to the number of years they had served in their respective bureau. The findings are shown in Table 5

Table 5 Experience

		Frequency	*Percent*	*Valid Percent*	*Cumulative Percent*
Valid	0-5 years	36	28.8	28.8	28.8
	6-10 year	41	32.8	32.8	61.6
	11-15 year	43	34.4	34.4	96.0
	16-20 year	5	4.0	4.0	100.0
				100.0	
Total		125	100.0		

Source: Field survey (2020)

According to the findings, 28.8% of the respondents had served for a period of 0-5 years, 32.8% of the respondents had served for a period of between 6-10 years, 34..4% of the respondents had served for a period of between 11-15 years while 4.0% of the respondents had served for a period of between 16-20 years. It was therefore concluded that majority of the respondents had been in the government long enough to understand issues relating to practices and challenges of women empowerment in public sectors.

4.1.5 Distribution of the respondent by Marital Status

The purpose of inquiring about the marital status of the respondents was to establish whether it had a positive or negative influence on their perception towards practices and challenges of women empowerment. The findings are shown in Table 6.

Table 6: Marital status

		Frequency	*Percent*	*Valid Percent*	*Cumulative Percent*
Valid	married	94	75.2	75.2	75.2
	single	31	24.8	24.8	100.0
				100.0	
Total		125	100.0		

Source: Field survey (2020)

The findings indicate that 75.2% of the respondents were married, 24.8. % of the respondents was single. This implies that the married respondents were the majority and were likely to understand the practices and challenges of women empowerment issues.

4.2 Dimension of women empowerment practices

This section basically needed to assess the level of women empowerment practices and challenges in public sectors. It was important in providing a clear understanding of the capacity of the respondents to embrace women empowerment. The domain factors were the extent of women Participation in Decision Making, the role of government in empowering women, the influence of Socio-cultural Status on women empowerment as presented in this section.

The practices of the Government program toward women empowerment

The study further sought to determine whether there was the influence in Socio-cultural Status on women empowerment practice. Table 7 presents the results of the findings.

Table 7: The practices of Government program toward women empowerment

Questions		*Measurement*						*Total*
		Scale	*SA*	*A*	*N*	*D*	*SD*	
1.	Education for girls can reduce early marriage	Frequency	84	19	4	12	6	125
		Percent	67.2	15.2	3.2	9.6	4.8	100.0
2.	Boys should be allowed to get more opportunity and resources for education than girls	Frequency	20	7	6	78	14	125
		Percent	16.0	5.6	4.8	62.4	11.2	100.0
3.	Women have equal chance of education with men	Frequency	90	9	11	10	5	125
		Percent	72.0	7.2	8.8	8.0	4.0	100.0
4.	Women empowerment can create self- confident and self-esteem for them	Frequency	23	73	8	12	9	125
		Percent	18.4	58.4	6.4	9.6	7.2	100.0
5.	Women participation and Motivation in political party and community activities is very high	Frequency	17	12	7	25	64	125
		Percent	13.6	9.6	5.6	20.0	51.2	100.0
6.	is a good idea to select woman to be office head in It government organization, for example, to be cabinet	Frequency	13	83	2	16	11	125
		Percent	10.4	66.4	1.6	12.8	8.8	100.0
7.	It is good idea to select a woman as community leader in your village, for example, kebel chairperson	Frequency	21	80	7	8	9	125
		Percent	16.8	64.0	5.6	6.4	7.2	100.0
8.	Economically, women have right to access control of resources in households level like land, income etc	Frequency	79	16	4	15	11	125
		Percent	63.2	12.8	3.2	12.0	8.8	100.0
9.	When a woman have small amount of money, such as 500-2000 birr, she has right to decide how to spent it by her own decision	Frequency	71	26	2	16	10	125
		Percent	56.8	20.8	1.6	12.8	8.0	100.0
10.	Women have right to buy clothes for herself or for children and sell things in the market without asking permission of her husband	Frequency	60	24	17	11	13	125
		Percent	48.0	19.2	13.6	8.8	10.4	100.0
11.	A woman have right to decide how to spent her free time on her own	Frequency	70	31	3	12	8	125
		Percent	56.0	24.8	2.4	9.6	7.2	100.0
12.	Girl should be allowed to wear whatever they want without being harassed	Frequency	8	80	7	20	10	125
		Per Percent	6.4	64.0	5.6	16.0	8.0	100.0

Source: Field survey (2020)

From the table 7 above, the majority of the respondents were strongly agrees/agrees with the statement that education for girls can reduce early marriage in the society which is indicated by 82.4%. 3.2% of the respondents have no opinion and the remaining 14.4% of the respondents were strongly disagree/ disagrees with the statement.

Boys should be allowed to get more opportunity and resources for education than girls, 21.6% of the respondents were strongly agree/agree, 4.8% of the respondents have no opinion and 73.6% of the respondents were strongly disagree/disagree. But most of the time, Women are involved in community managing role based on care and maintenance of human beings and provision of items of collective consumption, men on the other hand play a community leadership role in which they organize at the formal political level within the framework of structural system. This implies that women are involved in voluntary community activities in which they are not paid, while men are involved in a position of community leadership with paid capacity.

Moreover, 79.2% of the respondents were strongly agree/ agree with the statement 'Women have equal chance of education with men', 8.8% show no opinion and 12% of the respondents were strongly disagree/disagree.

Women empowerment can create self- confident and self-esteem for them, 76.8% of the respondents were strongly agree/agree while 6.4% have on sad on the statement and 16.8% of the respondents were strongly disagree/disagree. Women participation and Motivation in political party and community activities is very high. 23.2% of the respondents were strongly agree/agree, 5.6% of the respondents have no opinion and the remaining 71.2% of the respondents were strongly disagree/agree.

Is a good idea to select woman to be office head in It government organization, for example, to be cabinet,76.8% of the respondent were strongly agree/agree while 1.6% have on sad on the statement and 21.6% of the respondents were strongly disagree/disagree. It is good idea to select a woman as community leader in your village, for example, kebel chairperson 80.8% of the respondent were strongly agree/agree while 5.6% have on sad on the statement and 13.6 % of the respondents were strongly disagree/disagree.

Economically, women have right to access control of resources in households level like land, income etc 76% of the respondents were strongly agree/agree, 3.2% of the respondents have no opinion and the remaining 20.8% of the respondents were strongly disagree/ agree. When a woman have small amount of money, such as 500-2000 birr, she has right to decide how to spent it by her own decision 77.6% of the respondents were strongly agree/agree, 1.6% of the respondents have no opinion and the remaining 208% of the respondents were strongly disagree/agree.

Women have right to buy clothes for herself or for children and sell things in the market without asking permission of her husband 67.2% of the respondent were strongly agree/agree while 13.6% have on sad on the statement and 19.2% of the respondents were strongly disagree/disagree. 80.8 % of the respondents were strongly agree/agree, 2.4% of the respondents have no opinion and the remaining 16.8% of the respondents were strongly disagree/agree.

Girl should be allowed to wear whatever they want without being harassed,70.8% of the respondents were strongly agree/agree, 5.6% have no opinion and the remaining 24% of the respondents were strongly disagree/disagree.

4.2.2 Items related to the extent of challenges of Government program toward empowerment of women

The study determines whether there were challenges on women empowerment. Table 7 presents the results of the findings.

Table 8: The Challenges of Government program toward women empowerment

Questions		*Measurement*						*Total*
		Scales	*SA*	*A*	*N*	*D*	*SD*	
1.	Negative attitude toward women as a minor class in the society	Frequency	67	14	11	20	13	125
		Percent	53.6	11.2	8.8	16.0	10.4	100.0
2.	Lack of sufficient administration support from government Institutions	Frequency	28	63	7	10	17	125
		Percent	22.4	50.4	5.6	8.0	13.6	100.0

(Contd...)

3.	Lack of community awareness about the empowerment of women	Frequency	80	18	2	16	9	125
		Percent	64.0	14.4	1.6	12.8	7.2	100.0
4.	Lack of strong coordination mechanism of institutions to promote gender equality and empower women	Frequency	58	42	4	9	12	125
		Percent	46.4	33.6	3.2	7.2	9.6	100.0
5.	Due to capacity and others problem, national, legal instrument, local and declaration to ensure gender equality and human right have not been fully implemented	Frequency	7	80	4	24	10	125
		Percent	5.6	64.0	3.2	19.2	8.0	100.0

Source: Field survey (2020)

As it has been indicated in table 7, almost many respondents, 64.8 % of them were strongly agree/agree while 8.8% of them has no opinion and the remaining 26.4% of the respondents were strongly disagree/disagree. Similarly, the majority of the respondents 72.8% were strongly agree or agree with the statement that 'Lack of sufficient administration support from government Institutions ' while 5.6% of them have no opinion and 21.6 % of the respondents were strongly disagree or disagree with the statement.

Moreover, 78.4% of the respondents were strongly agree or agree with the statement that ' Lack of community awareness about the empowerment of women', 1.6% have no opinion and 20% of the respondents were strongly disagree/disagree.

Lack of strong coordination mechanism of institutions to promote gender equality and empower women 80% of the respondents were strongly agree/agree while 3.2% of them has no opinion and the remaining 16.8% of the respondents were strongly disagree/disagree.

Due to capacity and others problem, national, legal instrument, local and declaration to ensure gender equality and human right have not been fully implemented 69.6% of them were strongly agree/ agree while 3.2% of them has no opinion and the remaining 27.2% of the respondents were strongly disagree/disagree.

4.2.3 Item that related to the effects of Government practices toward women empowerment

The study determines whether there were challenges on women

empowerment. Table7 presents the results of the findings. Table 8 represented the finding

Table 9: The effects of Government practices toward women empowerment

	Questions	*Measurement*						*Total*
		Scales	*SA*	*A*	*N*	*D*	*SD*	
1.	Education for girls has many effects on development; such as reduction of child and maternal mortality, reduce early marriage	Frequency	90	12	3	12	8	125
		Percent	72.0	9.6	2.4	9.6	6.4	100.0
2.	When women are empowered, there may be higher productivity like income generation	Frequency	64	24	9	10	18	125
		Percent	51.2	19.2	7.2	8.0	14.4	100.0
3.	More education of women also be more and more women to attain leadership position at all level of the society	Frequency	80	15	5	15	10	125
		Percent	64.0	12.0	4.0	12.0	8.0	100.0
4.	When a women are empowered, it is helpful in conflict resolution	Frequency	80	11	6	25	3	125
		Percent	64.0	8.8	4.8	20.0	2.4	100.0

Source: Field survey (2020)

As it can be seen from table 8 above, the majority of respondents 81.6% were strongly agrees/agrees with the statement 'Education for girls has many effects on development; such as reduction of child and maternal mortality, reduce early marriage 'while 2.4% has no opinion and 16% of the respondents were strongly disagree/ disagree. Similarly, most of the respondents were strongly agree/ agree with the statement that; When women are empowered, there may be higher productivity like income generation rated by 70.4%, 7.2% have no say and 22.4% of the respondents were strongly disagree/disagree.

76 % of the respondents were strongly agrees/agrees with the statement 'also be more and more women to attain leadership position at all level of the society 'while 4.0% has no opinion and 20% of the respondents were strongly disagree/disagree.

72.8% of the respondents were strongly agrees/agrees with the statement 'When a women are empowered, it is helpful in conflict resolution 'while 4.8 % has no opinion and 22.4% of the respondents were strongly disagree/disagree.

4.2.4 Item that related to the extents of gender gap in socio-economic and demographic profiles

The study determines whether there was gender gap in socio-economic and demographic profiles. Table 9 presents the results of the findings.

Table 10: the extents of gender gap in some socio-economic and demographic profiles

Questions		*Measurement*						*Total*
		Scales	*SA*	*A*	*N*	*D*	*SD*	
1.	In households level, women are considered to be child rearing as well as other activity for family, like cooking, collecting fire wood, fetching water, washing clothes etc	Frequency	90	23	2	7	3	125
		Percent	72.0	18.4	1.6	5.6	2.4	100.0
2.	Women lower income and limited access to the resources like land, credit and assets, reduce an agreement power with in households	Frequency	60	25	7	10	23	125
		Percent	48.0	20.0	5.6	8.0	18.4	100.0
3.	In households level, girls can not allowed to school by their parents because of dowry payment	Frequency	83	27	2	8	5	125
		Percent	66.4	21.6	1.6	6.4	4.0	100.0
4.	Illiteracy and limited access to higher education affect the women participation in politic life in the societies	Frequency	70	28	4	3	20	125
		Percent	56.0	22.4	3.2	2.4	16.0	100.0
5.	Lack of production and community activity of women can also increase the gender gap in households as well as in the society	Frequency	65	20	12	10	18	125
		Percent	52.0	16.0	9.6	8.0	14.4	100.0

Source: Field survey (2020)

As it is can be seen from table 9 above, the majority of respondents 90.4% were strongly agrees/strongly agrees with the statement In households level, women are considered to be child rearing as well as other activity for family, like cooking, collecting fire wood, fetching water, washing clothes etc'. Whereas 1.6% has no opinion and 8 % of the respondents were strongly disagree/disagree.

Women lower income and limited access to the resources like land, credit and assets, reduce an agreement power with in households, 68% of the respondents were strongly agree/agree, 5.6% have no say and 26.4% of the respondents were strongly disagree/disagree.

In households level, girls can not allowed to school by their parents because of dowry payment 88% of the respondents were strongly agree/agree, 1.6% have no say and 10.4% of the respondents were strongly disagree/disagree. Illiteracy and limited access to higher education affect the women participation in politic life in the societies, 78.4 % of the respondents were strongly agree/agree, 3.2% have no say and 18.4% of the respondents were strongly disagree/disagree.

Lack of production and community activity of women can also increase the gender gap in households as well as in the society 68% of the respondents were strongly agree/agree, 9.6% have no say and 22.4% of the respondents were strongly disagree/disagree.

4.3 Discussions

Based on objective one infer that women employees working in the selected public sectors are not sufficiently represented in leadership position. It is further implied that, the majority of the respondents hardly believed that the women are posted/ represented uniformly across all public sectors at regional level. The analysis shows that women are not fairly represented in positions of greatest influence / legislative, executive, and judiciary organs. They argued that the women leaders are not as such active and exemplary model in making public decisions. Moreover, the respondents believed that the women leaders have no enough potential to guide, set the vision and to aspire other women to the position of leadership.

They also argued that women at different leadership positions are not full confident in decision making process. Finally, employees argued that women at senior level positions are not doing to empower other women i.e. coaching and, mentoring the future women leaders is less by the present women leaders. As interview conducted with Institution head of women, youth and children Affairs on (March 10, 2020) government public sectors at all levels are exerting much effort for the empowerment of women and encouraging progress has been registered as compared to the near futures. But in empowering women in leadership position still it need integrated effort of all stakeholders. The responses obtained from open ended question and document analysis also shows that, for the empowerment of women at leadership position, it needs the commitment of all concerned bodies, especially leaders at key leadership positions. From the findings, thus, one recognize that due attention should be given by all stakeholders to empower women at all levels of leadership positions.

Regarding objective two it is found that women in their organization women are not accessible to relevant training and development towards leadership. Although women have a clear understanding of the organizational mission and vision, the organization has no consistent plan to empower women as leaders there might be negative attitude to them. The analysis also implied that organization has not set any sustainable motivation system for women empowerment, attend and tries to fulfill the need which means that there was no community awareness about the women empowerment, and concern of women in leadership. Even tough, there are rules and regulations that indicates the women empowerment in the organizations, they are not encouraging and valuing the women employees for their creativity and contributions in leadership position. Furthermore, the leaders are not investing their time and energy in helping women to overcome weakness and improve their potential.

In addition, there is less emphasis for openly supporting successful mentoring relationships for leadership position of women; leaders are not committed to encourage women's overall development to become more good leaders. The data collected from the open-ended questions reveled that, the government has devoted to realize the equal participation and getting benefit from their involvement at all level, by designing polices and strategies that realize the benefit of women. But in reality women are not empowered to leadership positions. So, based on the above analysis, it can be said that leaders at top level and all the concerned bodies have to devote their time and energy to work cooperatively to empower women. From this it can be inferred that women are not expected to be leaders in the community due to a cultural impact.

Data analysis also tells that women are socially and culturally suffering from work stereotype and discrimination of labor because of the socio-cultural systems in the society. Women employees also argued that the job will be better done if the women lead the organization. Moreover, women are expected to be competent in acquiring the necessary leadership position. Therefore, there are cultural facts that influence the women involvement in empowerment. As the responses obtained from open-ended questions and interview of offices heads women are competent enough and devoted for their goals if they are not socially and culturally deprived from the chance of empowerment. From the findings, thus, one recognize that cooperative effort has to be taken by medias and all concerned bodies to raise the awareness in the community on the importance of empowering women.

With reference to objective three inferred that as a result of women empowerment, there are different activities that can help community especially in conflict resolution, women should be income generation and early marriage can be stopped. The analysis also shows that women believed that they have the ability to take risk of carrying burdens of their families even though there are cultural systems hindering their empowerment. It is also seen that because the women empowerment is less in the selected organizations, if they are empowered there might be high level of motivation to the resource ownership and development at the societal level.

Moreover, it is also found that even though the job of leaders is hard and takes huge amount of time, the women believed that family responsibilities are not barrier to women empowerment but there is the lack of concern for women empowerment from organizational side i.e. there is no mentoring, training, experience sharing, and development of women employees in the selected public sectors.

Finally, from objective four women believed that there are traditional beliefs and cultural attitudes in the society affecting the women's in decision making, women are considered as child rearing, fetching water, cooking food and collecting wild fire wood and other home activity. In the same way, the data obtained through the interviews made with the offices heads pointed out that women at top leadership positions are few in number almost they are one or two in number within the woreda.

Chapter Five

Conclusion and Recommendation

5.1 Conclusions

Based on the summary of major finding, the following conclusions have been drawn: this shows that there were no adequate measures taken for women's empowerment in leadership positions rate due to lack of strong coordination and attentions of politicians and governors officials. The challenges facing on the practice of women empowerment call for a serious concern especially in government public sectors.

Regarding demographic characteristics of the respondents, the study concluded that the lack of gender balance was a contributing factor to some of the challenges facing on the practice of women empowerment. Regarding experience, it was concluded that most respondents were in a position to understand the implication of gender issues since most of them had more than 5 years of experience working in the government public sectors and again most of them have certificate qualifications. Since most respondents were married, it was concluded that most of them were in a better position to appreciate women empowerment given that they relate with both males and females on a more personal level.

Based on objective one, the study concluded that the level of women participation political part and community activity was low in public sectors and hence hindered the process of practice of women empowerment. This was evidenced by failure of the government public sectors to adopt a women empowerment strategy which may have been as a result of lack of oversight by the government. This low level of participation was further linked to the lack of capacity building and gender awareness training which meant that the women employees were not equipped with necessary skills and knowledge to facilitate the practice of women empowerment.

Regarding objective two, this situation could also be attributed to failure by the government public sectors to integrate women empowerment into programmes. This gap was further widened by the fact that most respondents reported that they did not have the confidence to introduce gender issues at the workplace. The study concluded that despite the fact that the government had the capacity to access and mobilizes resource; the process was still ineffective in the practice of women empowerment. The government had an internal monitoring capacity and furthermore, funds were obtained from other bodies for the purpose of women empowerment. In addition, resource materials were adequate. Despite this capacity, government female employees did not get training opportunities to enhance their competence and neither did they have flexible terms, conditions and benefits for women who wanted to build their careers. If all these measures were in place, the process of women empowerment practice would be efficient especially when it came it human resource mobilization.

Moreover, there was no gender balance in interview panels and there was no gauging gender knowledge during interviews. The study thus concluded that the government did little to ensure that the right personnel to steer women empowerment were hired. The study had pointed out that human resources were integral for the practice of women empowerment.

In reference to objective three, the study concluded that ,the empowerment of women have many effects on development such as reduction of child and maternal mortality, reduce early marriage, increasing women participation in all aspect of thee development. But women are marginalized from decision making at all levels of public administration due to the lack of access to empowerment, the influence of traditional beliefs and cultural attitudes in society.

So, based on the above analysis, it can be said that all the concerned bodies have to work by integration to tackle the challenges of women empowerment practice, such as lack of access to participate in decision making position, getting relief from more responsibility to take risk of carrying burdens of their families, traditional beliefs and cultural attitudes in society influence women's in decision making and patriarchy systems interfered with the practice of women empowerment despite efforts by the government to discourage.

It was thus concluded that the government was not doing enough in terms of dealing with patriarchy systems all round. Moreover, it was concluded that the government was not keen on the progress of women who are the core of women empowerment given the inequalities they have faced over the years, the voice of women was not considered important in decision making processes. In addition, awareness was not created among female staff on the objectives of gender equality. Probably the government did not see the need. If the government was committed to the process of women empowerment, supervisors would have been encouraged to play a strong role in women empowerment to a large extent. Based on the findings, they were not encouraged to play a strong role in women empowerment practices.

In general, the study concluded that women are marginalized from decision making at all levels of public administration due to the lack of access to empowerment, the influence of traditional beliefs and cultural attitudes in society. So, based on the above analysis, it can be said that all the concerned bodies have to work by integration to tackle the challenges of women empowerment, such as lack of access to participate in decision making position, getting relief from more responsibility to take risk of carrying burdens of their families, traditional beliefs and cultural attitudes in society influence women's in decision making

5.2 Recommendations

The findings of this study revealed that the challenges are being faced on the practice of women empowerment in public sectors are: lack of community awareness, lack of access to strongly coordination among Government Institution to empower women, the influence of traditional beliefs and cultural attitudes in society, and dysfunctional policies, lack of access to participate in decision making position, getting relief from more responsibility to take risk of carrying burdens of their families, traditional beliefs and cultural attitudes in society influence women's in decision making.

To eradicate these challenges, the study recommended that capacity building; education and dissemination strategies should be adopted in government public sectors.

- The concept of women empowerment together with its dimensions is not well known as a strategy to realize gender equality in some public services sectors. Thus, much has to be done to introduce the concept to regional bureau heads/ deputies, woreda offices head, agencies directors, team leaders, experts and employees.

- The existing guidelines and framework plus relevance documents for women empowerment practice should be re-developed by the regional government administrative body in corporation with regional Women and Children Affairs Bureau up to woreda women and children affair office and distributed to the regional bureaus and agencies and woreda (district) offices in all public services sectors.

- The concept of women empowerment should be included in the functional adult literacy education program specially office of education and agriculture.

- Women and Children Affair Bureau should strengthen the awareness creation and make strong coordination system that can urged attention of leaders and experts on practice of women empowerment issues.

- One of the important experiences learned in this study is, the creation of "Gender Unit" in all public services sectors Institution to exercise leadership representation in the government structure even though there are gaps of knowledge, skills and capacity from women, this portrayed unique gender equality in the Gambella region. This experience should be transcended to the other regional state to materialize women's decision making role and thereby ensure gender equality.

- Another important result found in this study, is the concept of some head of bureaus, agencies directors and experts at regional and woreda public sectors women can be a cabinet or Office head, they have limited awareness on practice of women empowerment and this is the misconception that calls for strong intervention.
- In each public service sectors in the region and woreda, a qualified professional should be employed to monitor and technically support the women empowerment related activities.
- The administrative body responsible during budget allocation and break down should support and allocate the budget to public services sectors plans on women empowerment related activities.
- Prioritizing women needs and benefits in the economic development.
- Identification of risk factors to be address for political, social and development reforms.
- State administrative body should integrate women empowerment activities in GTP planning and program that can cascade and urge the sectors to speed up the women empowerment issues.
- Women units in each public services sector should be given training especially in the dimension of women empowerment strategies and guideline specially the Gambella prosperity party (GPP) must take lead to work on it to improve their knowledge on adopted gender policy, strategy and program in regional up to woreda public services sector on how to practice women empowerment activities.
- Policy implementers especially top line leaders and middle line management need trainings on attitudinal changes of their perception on women empowerment practice; this seriously

call for attention of WCA, regional council and regional administrative body to take leads on this issues.

- In addition to that, advocacy should be conducted among traditional leaders and authorities to integrate gender issues in their work so as to address all known cultural issues that hinder the practice of women empowerment.

References

- Almaz, E (1991).Perspective on Gender and Development. In TsehaiBerhaneSelassie(Ed)
- Gender Issue in Ethiopia.Institute of Ethiopian Studies. AddisAbaba University, Addis Ababa.
- Aspy, C.B. &Sandhogs, D.S. (1999). Empowering women for equity: counseling Approach.America nCounseling Association, Alexandria, VA. 22304.
- BalkD.199.DefyinggendernormsinruralBangladesh: A social demographic analysis.Population Studies, 51:153-172.
- Balk D (1994).Individual and community aspects of women's status and fertility In rural Bangladesh. Population Studies, 48 (1): 21-45.
- Batliwala, S. (1995).Meaning of women's empowerment. Women's World, 23-34.
- Bennett,L. (2002). Using Empowerment and Social Inclusi on for Propoor Growth: A theory of Social Change. Working Draft of Background Paper for the Social Development Strategy Paper. Washıng: World Bank.
- Bhadra, B. (2001).Janani O Prayukti: Lingakaran O Kshama-tayaner Sahabastan.(Bengali Ed.) Yojana.
- Bhasin, K. (1998). Why empower in gwomen. In Sushama Sahay (ed.), Women and Empowerment: Approaches and Strategies, Discovery Publishing House, New Delhi.

- Biswas, S.K. (2010).New Tribal Panchayat in Nicobar Islands. Kurukshetra, Ministry of Rural Development, New Delhi.
- Blanchard, K. H., John P. Carlos, & Randolph, A. (1996). Empowerment takes more than a minute. San Francisco: Berrett-Koehler.
- Brill, A. (ed.) (2000). A rising public voice: Women in politics worldwide. New York, UNIFEM.
- Carpenter. And Egerton, J (2007).Working in partnership through early Support: Family structure (Distance Learning Text).
- Chandra, S.K.(1997).Women and empowerment.Indian Journal of Public Administration,July-Sept.
- Carr.M. (2000).Women's economic empowerment: key to development. In Women's Empowerment and Economic Justice; Reflecting on Experience in Latin America and the Caribbean, De Pauli L (Ed). UNIFEM: New York.
- Chattopadhyay, A. (2005). Women and entrepren-eurship.Yojana, a Monthly Journal of Ministry of Information and Broadcasting, 5(1), New Delhi.
- C, theme. A (2005).the context of Women Health Survey: Result from the Demographic and
- Health Survey, 1994-2001.ComparativeReport No 11Calvert on, Maryland: ORC Marco.
- Devendra, K. (2001). Whose empowerment are we talking of: Women! But where will we find our Girls" In Promilla Kapur (ed.), Empowering the Indian Women. Publications Division, Ministry Of Information and Broadcasting, Government of India, New Delhi.
- Djakarta Declaration. (June 7-14, 1994). For the advancement of women in Asia and the Pacific.Second Asian and Pacific Ministerial Conference on Women in Development Education Sector Development Program I-IV.
- Elliott,C.M. (2008). Global empowermen to fwomen: Res ponses to globalization and Politicized Religions. Routledge, New York.

- FAO (Food and Agriculture Organization of the United Nations). 2011. The State of Food and Agriculture. Womenin Agriculture. Lancet (2).Rome.Retrievedfromwww.fao.org/docrep/013/i2050e/i2050e.pdf.
- FDRE (1994).Cultural Policy. Addis Ababa: Artistic Printing Press. Federal Civil Service Commission (2005).Survey on the Status of Men and Women Employees and Strategies for Gender Equality. Main Report. Addis Ababa.
- FDRE.1994. Constitution off ederal democraticre public of Ethiopia Golla, A.M, Mhalhotra, A.N and a Pand Mehra, R.2011. Understanding and measuring Women Economic empowerment: Definition, Framework an international center for Research on Women (ICRW).
- Gangrade, K.D.(2001). Gandhi and empowermen to fwomen: Milestogo in Promilla Kapur (ed.), Empowering the Indian Women, New Delhi: Ministry of Information and Broadcasting, Government of India.
- Helina, Beyene (2015). Final Report National Assessment: Ethiopia Gender Equality and the Knowledge Society. https://owsd.net/sites/default/files/National%20Assessment%20on%20Gender% 20and%20STI%20-%20Ethiopia.pdf.
- Hindin, M.J (2000). Women power and anthro pometric statusin Zimbabwe. Soc. Sci.Med, 51:15171528
- Hirut,T. (2004). Violence Against Women in Ethiopia: A strong case of civil so ciety concern. In: chowdhury, S., Wais, A., and KhahsaWoldeGis (eds) civil society in Ethiopia: Reflectionon Reality and Perspective of Hope. African-Asian Studies Promotion Association.
- Jejeebhoy SJ, 2000, Women's autonomy in rural India: Its dimensions, determinants and the influence of context. In:Women's empowerment and demographic Processes, Harriet Banda Gita Sen Presser. New York: Oxford University Press.
- Jelaludin a, Abgeli a, Alemtsehay B, Salvini S (2001).Gender Issues, Population and Development in Ethiopia: in-depth Studies

from the 1994 Population and Housing Census in Ethiopia Central Statistical Authority, Addis Ababa, and Institute fo rPopulation Research National Research Council (Irp - Cnr), Roma.

- Jejeebhoy SJ, Sathar ZA (2001). Women's autonomy in Indiaand Pakistan: TheinfluenceofReligion and region. Population and Development Review, 27(4): 687-712.
- Kabeer,N. (2005). Gender equality and Women empowerment: criticalanalysis of the third Millennium Develop ment goal1 Gender Devel.13, 13-24.
- Kapur, P. (2001). Empowering the Indian Women. Publications Division, Ministry of Information and
- Broadcasting, Government of India, NewDelhi. Ritz MM, Makinwa Adebusoye P,
- GurakDT (2000).The role of gender context in Shaping Reproductive behavior in Nigeria. In: Women's empowerment and demographic Processes, Harriet B. and
- Gita Sen Presser. New York: Oxford University Press.Mukuria A, Abuolfia Langley, E., & Fox, V.C.(1994). Women's rights in the United States: A documentary history (eds).West Port, Connecticut: Winston Greenwood Pres.
- Leah, L. (2002). (Reprint), Humanrights: Questions and answers.NationalBookTrust, Indian Collaboration with UNESCO Publishing, New Delhi.
- Manohar, S. (2001).Human rights for women's empowerment. In Promilla Kapur (ed.) Empowering the Indian Women, Publications Division, Ministry of Information and Broadcasting, Government of India, New Delhi
- Mohanty, B. (1999).Panchayati Raj institutions and women. In Bharati Roy & Aparna Basu (eds.), From Independence towards Freedom. Indian Women since 1947.Oxford University Press, New Delhi.
- Niroj, S. (2000).Women in Indian politics. New Delhi: Gyan Publishing House.

- Office of the Prime Minister.1993.National Policy of Ethiopian Women: the Transitional Government of Ethiopia (Women'saffairsector), AddisAbaba.12.
- Oxford Policy Management, 2013.Gualitative Research and analysis of the economic Impact of Cash transfer program in sub-Saharan African: Research guide for the protection to production (PtoP) program.FAO, Rome.Pathak, S.B., (Dy. Director), Panchayati Raj Directorate, Jharkhand, Ranchi, India, Personal interview on14th August, 2003.
- Patricia S.E. Darlington & Mulvaney, B. M. (2003).Women power and ethnicity Working
- Toward Reciprocal empowerment. The Haworth Press, New York London, Oxford.
- Prasad, R.R. (2002).Participation and empowerment-rhetoric and realities. Kurukshetra, a Journal on Rural Development, New Delhi.
- Rajput, P. (2001). Women's political participation in India: Anagendaforempowerment. In PromillaKapur (ed.), Empowering the Indian Women, New Delhi, Ministry of
- Information and Broadcasting, Government of India
- Rao, P.H.S ethumadhav. (2001). Education for women's empowerment. In Promilla Kapur (ed.), Empowering the Indian Women. Public ations Division, Ministry of In formation and Broadcasting, Government of India, New Delhi.
- Sahay, S. (1998).Women and empowerment: Approaches and strategies. Discovery Publishing House, New Delhi.
- Schuler SR, Hashemi SM, 1994, Credit programs, women's empowerment, and contraceptive use in rural Bangladesh. Studies in Family Planning, 25(2):65-76.
- Sharma, K. (199192).Grassroot sorganizations and women'sempowerment: Some issues in the contemporary debate. In Samya Shakti, Centre for Women's Development Studies, New Delhi.

- Shiva, M. (2001).Health care in last 50 years and women's empowerment. In PromillaKapur (ed.), empowering the Indian Women.Publications Division, Ministry of Information and Broadcasting, Government of India, New Delhi.
- Tiwari, R.S.(2001).Feminism and globalization versus Indian women empowerment. In AbhaAvastiand A.K.Srivastava (eds.), Modernity, Feminism and Women's Empowerment, RawatPublication, New Delhi.
- United Nations (2005), Progress Towards the Millennium Development Goals, 1990-2005, Secretary-General's Millennium Development Goals Report. June 13, 2005.
- UN Women. 2014. Preliminary Gender profile of Ethiopia. Addis Ababa.
- Verba, S. & Nie, N.H. (1972). Participation in America: Political democracy and social equality.

Acronyms

CEDAW	:	Cambridge Emergence and Displacement Group
ECOSO	:	Economic and Social council
FAO	:	Food and Agricultural Organization
FDRE	:	Federal democracy Republic of Ethiopia
GER	:	Gross Enrolment Ratio
MDG	:	Millennium Development Goals
UDHR	:	Universal declaration of Human right
UN	:	United Nation
UNFPA	:	United Nation for Population Activities
UNIFEM	:	United Nation Development Fund for Women
WB	:	World Bank
WEP	:	Women empowerment Program
MOWCSA	:	Minister of Women, Children and Social Affair
WHO	:	World Health Organization

Index

Z